# PORTUGUESE SOUL FOOD

## BlueRooster

PublishAmerica
Baltimore

First printing

PublishAmerica has allowed this work to remain exactly as the author intended, verbatim, without editorial input.

Hardcover 9781462667819
PUBLISHED BY PUBLISHAMERICA, LLLP
www.publishamerica.com
Baltimore

Printed in the United States of America

# Acknowledgments

I would like to thank my mom Ana, for inspiring me to write this book. Her love for Portuguese food, made me realize that it's more than food. It's seating at the dinner table with your family and friends and have a good time. She also made me realize that being Portuguese was not such a bad thing.

Thank you to my dear husband Josh. There is no better and talented husband than my husband. He keeps me inspired every single day. Without his support and love I would never be able to write this book. Not forgetting that his cooking warms my heart and my soul, every single time. Thank you for being my best friend.

Thanks to my munchkins Gabriella and Jordan. You are the light of my life. Cannot imagine life without you.

And, to the rest of my family that gave me love, strength and inspiration to do write this book. Thanks.

Love you all.

# INTRODUCTION

## *My Portuguese Roots*

Born and raised for the first years of my life in the north of Portugal, in a small city called Chaves "City of the Keys". I learned to love the food, people and all the culture that North of Portugal has to offer. Chaves "City of the Keys".

The geographic aspects of the Town of Chaves "Keys," of the district of Village Real, its situated in the edges of the river Tâmega, in the border of the north of the province of the Galiza (Spain).

The river Tâmega, important tributary of the Douro, since always influenced the development of town, for the valley where it runs, and for the fertile valley that crosses. The town of Chaves occupies an area of 591,3 km2, in which if they distribute 51 villages: Vilela Seca, etc…

In 2005 Town presented 43 667 inhabitants. Natural or the inhabitant of Chaves calls itself flaviense "from the Latin Aqua Flavie". History and the construction of Monuments that retrace to Daily pay-History, Chaves were busy for the Romans, the Barbarians and the Moors, only being considered Portuguese City in century XI. Of its important archaeological patrimony the medieval castle of Chaves and its opponent tower of house arrest under bail are distinguished; the bridge

Roman of Keys—Bridge of Trajano; the first church was built and the Castle of Monforte of the Free River in Cold Waters.

Tourism is one of the more important economic activities in Town, nominated with the Spas of Chaves (Caldas de Chaves), where the water leaves the 73 ºC, being hottest of the Iberian Peninsula. The cattle creation swine, base of the famous hams of Chaves, is also another activity to consider. It stops beyond would sausages "salsicharia", the industrial activity and artisan very it is associated with ceramics and the production of blankets.

The crossroads of road communications for Braga, Bragança and Spain, the attraction exerted for the spas, associates to the tourism, and intense commercial activity e, in some dominions, industrial discloses to the economic dynamism of this Town.

# A QUICK PORTUGUESE GASTRONOMIC

## *Tour of the Tras-os-Montes "Behind the Mountains" region*

The region of Tras-os-Montes "behind the Mountains" and Alto Douro is placed north-eastern of continental Portugal, corresponding to the districts of Village Real and Bragança, as well as the four Counties of the district of Viseu and to one of the district of Guarda. It makes border with Spain, the north and the east, and confines with the provinces of the High Side, the south, and of the Coastal Douro and the Minho, the west. The relief of this region is formed by a set of high wavy platforms cut for valleys and very deep basins. Its climate is Mediterranean with continental influence, more wasteland and cold in the planate areas, hotter in the incased deep areas of the Douro. Beyond the vine—in special the vine of the Demarcated Region of the wine of the Port, where the landscape if individualized with its immense hillsides and fifth—, it produces cultures like rye, barley and potatoes. This region presents, in its main typical plates, the bread; cod, sausages "alheiras", ham and heifer, with prominence for the mirandesa ece of fish, river fish "mostly trout". It also produces broccoli rave, beans, mushrooms and chestnuts. Also know for their breads, cheeses, cakes, and pastries among others.

In place of lush green vegetation, dense forests, and scraggy bush suitable for herds of sheep, goats, cows and pigs cover this desolated and punishingly untamed region.

This is meat country. Well known for their meats in Portugal, has well worldwide.

# CONTENTS

# STARTERS

*Salt Cod Fritters*
*Chicken Turnovers*
*Goat Cheese Salad*
*Mussels in an Iron Pot*
*Grilled Shrimp with Piri-piri Sauce*
*Asparagus with "Presunto" Ham*
*Green Salad with Olives*

# Salt Cod Fritters

- 1Lbs of Yukon potatoes, peeled and cut into cubes
- 3 Tbsp of Olive Oil
- 10 Oz Salt Cod, soaked, cooked and flaked
- 1 Tsp of paprika (or store-bought hot sauce to taste)
- 3 Tbsp of fresh flat-leaf parsley, finely minced
- 1 to 2 large eggs (for more dense fritters use one eggs)
- Salt and pepper to taste
- Vegetable oil, for frying

1—Plunk the potatoes into a large pot with water salt, cover, and bring to a boil. Cook until tender, 20minutes. Drain, dump the potatoes into a bowl, and mash them well. Set aside, uncovered.

2—Drop the cooked cod into a food processor and pulse until finely shredded. I flake the cod with my hands, this way I make sure that no bones go into the mixture.

3—Add cod into the potatoes bowl, along with the paprika, fresh parsley, salt, pepper and eggs. Mix well and taste.

4—Heat 2 inches of oil in a saucepan with high sides, until it reaches 350 degrees. Meanwhile, grab two tablespoons; scoop a tablespoon of the cod mixture and role them between the two spoons until you make a small footballs (looks like a miniature of a football).

5—Place a few of the balls into the oil and fry in batches of 5 or 6, until golden brown, about 3 minutes. Fish out the fritters and transfer them to paper towels. Sprinkle with fresh parsley and serve warm.

You can also serve them cold. They last up to three months in the freezer

# Chicken Turnovers

**For the dough:**
- 1 Cup of water
- 2 Tbsp of butter cut in pieces
- 2 Cups all purpose flour, plus more for dusting

**For the filling:**
- 3 Tbsp of olive oil
- ½ Lbs of chicken breast, minced or ground
- 1 Medium onion, minced
- 2 Garlic cloves, minced
- ¼ Cup of olives, pitted and cut in small pieces
- ¼ Cup of chicken broth
- ½ Tbsp of fresh parsley, minced

**For frying:**
- 2 Large eggs
- 2 Cups of breadcrumbs
- Vegetable oil for frying

1—Heat the olive oil in a large skillet or wok over medium heat until hot. Lower the heat to medium-low and add onion, garlic, chicken and cook, breaking up the meat with a wooden spoon, stirring frequently. Add broth and let it simmer, until broth evaporates almost completely.

2—Remove saucepan form the heat and season chicken with salt, pepper, olives and fresh parsley and set aside and let it cool completely.

3—Heat the water, butter, slat in a medium saucepan over medium—low eat until wisps of steam curl up. Lower the heat to low, dump in the flour ½ cup a t the time, and immediately beat the mixture with a wooden spoon, until the dough cooks through and pulls away from the pan, around 3 minutes. Transfer dough to a floured work surface.

4—To assemble the turnovers, set a side a glass of water, teacup or you can cut it with a cookie cutter. Roll the dough into a ball and cut it in half, keeping it covered. Roll out the one half with a roller pin; keep it dry, until 1/18 inch thick. Cut the dough in circles,

(Cut circles one at the time) with the glass and dollop a teaspoon of the chicken mixture in each dish. Fold the turnover in half, and crop the edges with your fingers or fork. Repeat until finish.

5—Heat the vegetable oil in a medium saucepan or fryer with high sides, until it reaches 350 degrees. Keep eat constant temperature of 350 degrees, otherwise, the turnover may burn.

6—Wisk eggs in a bowl, place breadcrumbs in a plate. Pass the turnover in the egg, breadcrumbs, and place 4 to 5 turnovers into the oil. Fry, turning over frequently, until golden brown, 3minutes per side. Transfer to paper towels. Before serving sprinkle the turnovers with fresh parsley. These can be served warm, room temperature or cold. Most of people like them warm.

# GOAT CHEESE SALAD

- 3 Brunches of fresh Thyme, minced
- 3 Brunches of fresh rosemary, minced
- 1 Garlic clove, minced
- 8 Tbsp of olive oil
- 8 Slices of French bread, or artisan
- 8 Slices of fresh Goat cheese, about 40 grams each
- 1 Small arugula
- 1 Small lettuce
- ½ Cup of cherry tomatoes cut in half
- 2 Tbsp of white vinegar, or balsamic
- ¼ Black olives, pitted, cut in half

1—Wash, and mince thyme, rosemary and garlic. Sauté the mixture in 4 tbsp of olive oil, add the bread, until golden brown. Remove bread, put in a serving dish, and set aside.

2—Wash arugula, lettuce and cherry tomatoes. Cut tomatoes in half, reap lettuce with your hand, or cut it in small pieces. Put the

White wine vinegar, salt, pepper, olives, and the 4 remaining tbsp of olive oil, in a bowl and mix it together.

3—Grill the goat cheese, 2 minutes both sides, place it on top of the bread. Add salad mixture and drizzled with white wine dressing. Serve warm.

# Mussels in an Iron Pot

- 2 Lbs of Fresh mussels
- 2 Large onions cut thin
- 2 Medium carrots cut in circles
- ¼ Head of celery, minced
- ½ Head of French garlic, minced
- ½ Cup of white wine
- 3 Tbsp of olive oil
- 1 Bunch of fresh parsley, minced
- 2 Tbsp of fresh rosemary
- 2 Laurel leaves
- Salt and pepper to taste

1—Wash the mussels with running cold water, until no more sand comes out of the mussels. Discard the open mussels, keeping only the closed ones.

2—Heat the olive oil in a large Iron pot. Add onions, carrots, celery, French garlic, rosemary, laurel leaves, ¼ cup of parsley, wine, salt and pepper to taste. Put mussels into the iron pot, cover them with water, cover and let them boil until open.

3—Mussels are ready when open; disregard any mussels that didn't open. Remove mussels from the heat and let them rest for 5 minutes before serving. Serve the mussels with broth in deep soup bowls and drizzle with fresh parsley. Not forgetting the artesian whole wheat bread, for dipping, with butter.

# Grilled Shrimp with Piri-piri Sauce

- 20 Large shrimp, peeled and devein
- 2 Tbsp of butter, melted
- 2 Tsp of vegetarian seasoning
- 4 Large onions cut in fourths
- 4 Cloves of garlic cut in half
- 1 Tbsp of olive oil
- 3 Tbsp of chicken broth
- 2 Tbsp of balsamic vinegar
- 1 Package of bacon, thin (turkey bacon works as well)
- Salt and pepper to taste

1—Peel shrimp and devein them. Melt butter, let it cool, and brush shrimp with it. Drizzle the shrimp with the seasoning.

2—Cut onions in fourths and garlic in half's. Put shrimp in wood skewers, alternating with onions, garlic and bacon.

3—Put skewers I the grill, turning them often, 8 minutes per side. Mix the olive oil, chicken broth, seasoning and brush shrimp often with this mixture. Serve with a fresh salad or Cole saw.

# Asparagus with "Presunto" Ham

- 1 Lbs of green asparagus
- 1 Tbsp of butter
- 12 Slices ham, thin slices
- 1 Bunch of parsley
- 2 Tbsp of honey
- 3 Tbsp of olive oil
- 1 Tbsp of balsamic vinegar

1—Wash the asparagus and disregard the bottom. Put them in a large pan and cook in water. Add salt, butter and sugar and let it cook for 10 to 15 minutes until all dente.

2—Take asparagus out of the pan, refresh in cold water and drain. Enroll 2 asparagus in a slice of ham. Arrange in a decorative rolls on a platter.

3—With the blender prepare a sauce with parsley, honey, olive oil and balsamic vinegar. Serve asparagus warn and accompanied with this sauce.

# GREEN SALAD WITH OLIVES

- 2 Tbsp of sweet wine
- 2 Tbsp of red wine vinegar
- 4 Tbsp of olive oil
- 1 Tsp of mustard
- 1 Tsp of salt
- 1 Tsp of pepper
- 100 g Raisins
- 150 g Sheep's cheese
- 200g Black olives (no pits)
- 500 g Hearts of palm
- 1 Head of red lettuce
- 1 Tbsp Fresh Basil

1—Prepare sauce by mixing the sweet wine, vinegar, olive oil, mustard, salt and pepper. Wash the raisins in hot water, grind up the cheese, cut olives into slices and put aside.

2—Wash the Palmetto dry them and cut into circles.

Separate the lettuce leaves. In a serving bowl mix lettuce, palmetto, olives, raisins and sprinkle it with the sauce.

Serve garnished with fresh basil.

# SOUPS

*Portuguese Pumpkin Soup*
*Vovo Ana's Vegetable Soup*
*Creamy Soup of Fish*
*Carrot and Ginger Soup Portuguese Style*
*Portuguese Green Soup with Chorizo*
*My Father's Favorite Fava Bean Soup*

# PORTUGUESE PUMPKIN SOUP

- 1 Lbs of Pumpkin, peeled, cut in cubes
- 2 Medium onions, minced
- 2 Garlic cloves, minced
- 3 Tbsp of olive oil
- ½ Cup of dry white wine
- 3 Cups of vegetable or chicken broth
- 1 Egg white
- 250 g of fresh cheese
- 1 Tbsp of cornstarch
- ½ Tsp of cayenne pepper
- ½ Cup of heavy cream
- 2 Tbsp of pumpkin seed oil

1—Peel and cut pumpkin into cubes. Heat oil in a saucepan, add onions, garlic, and pumpkin and let them cook for about 5 minutes, until golden brown.

2—Add wine, vegetable or chicken broth, cover and let them cook in low heat, for about 30minutes.

3—Meanwhile, whisk the egg white in a bowl until fluffy. Add cheese, cornstarch, salt and cayenne pepper, and mix well. With a tablespoon make small balls and cooked them in boiling water and salt, for about 12 minutes.

4—Remove the pumpkin from heat and puree it in batches in the food processor, salt and pepper to taste. Return soup to a low heat, adding the heavy cream, salt, pepper, mixing often, and let it cook for about 10 minutes.

5—Serve soup with the cheese balls, and drizzle with Pumpkin seed oil. This soup tastes better when hot.

# Vovo Ana's Vegetable soup

- 1 Large onion, minced
- 3 Medium Yukon potatoes, peeled and cut into cubes
- 2 Medium carrots, peeled and cute into ¼ discs
- 1 Bunch of celery, cut into cubes
- 2 Medium zucchinis cut into discs
- 4 Tbsp of butter
- 2 Tbsp of fresh parsley, minced
- 5 Cups of vegetable or chicken broth
- Salt and pepper

1—Peel and wash onions, garlic, zucchini, celery, carrots and potatoes. In a large saucepan add butter and let it melt. Add vegetables to the saucepan and let them cook for about 5 minutes, mixing often.

2—Add vegetable or chicken broth to the saucepan and let it cook, in a medium heat, for about 30 minutes. The vegetables should be cooked all dente.

3—Add salt and pepper to the soup and drizzled with fresh parsley.

# CREAMY SOUP OF FISH

- 1 Lb of white fish fillets
- 1 Medium onion, cubes
- 2 Garlic cloves, cubs
- 4 Medium potatoes, peeled, sliced 1/16 inch
- 3 Tbsp of butter
- 1 Can of San Marzano tomatoes
- ½ Cup of fresh parsley, minced
- 2 Laurel leaves
- 1 Tsp of cayenne pepper
- 2 ½ Cups of fish or vegetable broth
- ½ Cup of heavy cream
- Fennel for serving

1—Cut the fish, onions and garlic into cubes. Peel potatoes and cut them into very thin slices.

2—Melt butter in a saucepan. Add onions, garlic and potatoes, mixing often. Add ½ cup of water, cover, and let it simmer for 10 minutes.

3—Add fish, tomatoes, parsley, laurel leaves, fish or vegetable broth and let it simmer for, 8 more minutes. Mix heavy cream to the soup, salt and pepper and let it simmer for 5 more minutes.

4—Remove laurel leaves. Decorate soup with the fennel and serve it warm with toasted bread.

# CARROT AND GINGER SOUP PORTUGUESE STYLE

- 1 Medium onion, minced
- 2 Garlic cloves, minced
- 3 Medium carrots, diced
- 1 Bunch of celery, diced
- 1 Small root of fresh ginger, shaved
- 2 Tbsp of Olive Oil
- 6 Cups of vegetable or chicken broth
- ½ Bunch of fresh cilantro
- 2 Tbsp of heavy cream
- Salt and pepper to taste

1—Peal the onions, garlic, carrots, celery and cut them. Peal ginger and shaved it.

2—Put the olive oil in a deep pan, onions, garlic and let them get medium brown. Add carrots, ginger, celery and cook for another 5minutes, mixing often. Add vegetable or chicken broth, cover, and let it cook in a medium low heat, for 30 minutes.

3—Puree the soup, with a food processor or hand blender, until smooth, no lumps. Wash the cilantro, minced, add it to the soup. Salt and pepper to taste. Let it simmer for 5 more minutes. Serve soup warm and decorate with heavy cream.

# Portuguese Green Soup with Chorizo

- 1 Large onion, chopped
- 1 Lbs of Yukon potatoes, peeled and diced
- 3 Garlic cloves, diced
- 5 Cups of chicken or vegetable broth
- 1 Bunch of collard greens, remove,
- thick center stems and fibrous veins
- 6 Tbsp of olive oil
- 1 Small Linguica, or dry-cured smoked sausage,
- cut into ¼ inch thick slices

1—Heat the Olive oil in a large pot over medium low heat. Add onion, garlic and cook, until light brown, about 7 minutes. Dump potatoes and cook for another 3 minutes.

2—Pour in the chicken broth and bring to a boil over high heat. Reduce heat to medium low, cover and let it simmer until the potatoes follow apart, 20 minutes.

3—Meanwhile, wash the collard greens, stack several collard leafs, and roll them lengthwise into a tight shape. Cut, collard greens into very thin slices, repeat until finish.

4—Puree the soup using a handheld blender. Return it to the pot, add collard greens, a few slices of linguica, and bring it back to a simmer, 5 minutes.

5—Serve soup in a deep bowl, crown each bowl with 4 or 5 slices of linguica and drizzle some olive oil.

# Fava Bean Soup

- 3 Lbs of fresh Fava beans, shelled
- 2 Tbsp of olive oil
- 1 Large Onion, diced
- 2 Medium Yukon potatoes, peeled, diced
- 6 Cups of chicken or vegetable broth
- 1 Small shallot, cut into ½ inch
- Salt and pepper to taste

1—Bring a large pot of water and salt to a boil. Add Fava beans and let them cook for about 5 minutes. Dump the beans and rinse with cold water, before peeling.

2—Heat the oil in a large pot over medium heat. Add onions, potatoes and cook, stirring often, for about 10 minutes. Pour in the chicken or vegetable broth, cover, bring to a boil, and cook until potatoes are tender, about 5 to 7 minutes.

3—Add Fava beans to the soup. Using a handheld blender puree the soup until smooth. Pass it trough a mesh for a smoother texture. Salt and pepper to taste.

4—Serve soup warm in shallow bowls. Top with shallots and Fava beans, drizzle with olive oil.

# FISH AND SHELFISH

*Grill Trout*
*Grill Sardines with Peppers*
*Mussels in a Curry Sauce*
*Sea Bass with Fennel and Citrus Sauce*
*Cod with Cabbage*
*Cod "a Gomes de SA" with Eggs*
*Cod "a Bras" with Fries*

# GRILL TROUT

- 4 Trout's, clean, ready to cook
- 4 Branches of fresh rosemary
- 12 Slices of Bacon
- 6 Medium mushrooms
- 2 Tbsp of olive oil
- ½ Tsp of dry thyme
- 1 Tsp of sweet chili
- 1 Lemon juice
- Salt and pepper to taste

1—Dry Trout with paper towels inside and out. Rub trout's with salt, and lemon juice. Put rosemary inside the trout and wrap them with the bacon, secure them with toothpicks, if necessary.

2—Clean mushrooms with a wet clothe, and mix them with olive oil, thyme, salt and lemon juice. Meanwhile turn own the oven at 350 degrees.

3—Place trout's with mushrooms in a wire hamper, and grill them for a bout 5 minutes each side. Until bacon it's crispy. Dust Trout's and mushrooms with sweet chili and serve warm.

# Grill Sardines with Peppers

- 6 to 8 Sardines, clean, no scales
- 4 Green or red peppers
- 4 Tbsp of olive oil
- 2 Garlic cloves, diced
- 1 small onion (optional) cut in half moons
- Fresh Parsley
- Salt and pepper to taste

1—Clean and scale sardines, dry them inside out with paper towels. Rub them with some olive oil, salt and pepper.

2—Put peppers in a hot grill and turn them over every 2 minutes, total of 8 minutes. After removing them from the grill tries to peel them, they will be very <u>hot,</u> set them aside with salt, garlic and olive oil.

3—Grill sardines for about 10 minutes. Serve them warm with the grill peppers and fresh parsley. Grandpa also likes some raw onion with the grill sardines along with whole wheat bread.

# Mussels in a Curry Sauce

- 6 Lbs of mussels, scrubbed and rinsed
- 1 ½ cup of white wine
- 2 Medium Vidalia onions
- 3 Garlic cloves, minced
- 3 Medium tomatoes, seeded, cored and chopped
- 2 Tbsp of curry powder
- 2-3 Tbsp of piri-piri or hot sauce
- 4 Tbsp of olive oil
- 4 Cup of rice, preferable cooked
- 1 Tsp of ground ginger
- 3 Tbsp Fresh cilantro, chopped
- Salt and pepper to taste

1—Heat the oil in a skillet over medium low heat, until it shimmers. Add onions, garlic and cook for about 7 minutes. Stir in the tomatoes, curry powder, ginger, and cook, stirring constantly until fragrant, 4 minutes. Set aside.

2—Discard any Mussels that feel heavy, broken or don't close when tapped. Put the wine in a large and deep pot and. clatter in the mussels, cover and let it cook for about 15 minutes, until shells pop open (disregard the ones that refuse to open). Strain the mussel's liquid.

3—Pluck some of the mussels from their shells and add them to the tomato mixture, with ½ cup of the mussel's liquid. Let them cook in a low heat for about 5 minutes. Take the pan of the heat and mixture the rest of the mussels.

4—Serve mussels over rice. Add salt, pepper and piri-piri sauce to taste.

# Sea Bass with Fennel and Citrus Sauce

- 2 Sea Bass, fresh and clean
- 4 Tbsp of olive oil
- 1 Small fennel bulb, cored and thinly sliced
- 2 Large oranges
- 2 Medium lemons
- 2Tbsp fresh cilantro
- ¼ Cup of white wine
- Salt and pepper to taste

1—Pre-heat the oven at 350 degrees. You should have 1/3 cup of juice from one orange. Set aside. Wash, clean and dry Sea Bass inside out with paper towels. Brush Sea Bass with olive oil and orange juice, add salt and pepper to taste.

2—Cut 1 orange and the 2 lemons into circles. Wash fennel, cilantro and let them dry a bit. Place in the Sea Bass belly 2 slices of orange, 3 of lemon, fennel and cilantro. Tie Sea Bass with cooking string. Sprinkle the rest of the orange juice and olive oil on top of the fish and herbs.

3—Place Sea Bass in the oven and let it cook for about 40 minutes. Mix white wine and orange juice and brush fish every 6 to 8 minutes on both sides, until cooked. Remove string and serve warm with the rest of the herbs, oranges and lemons.

# COD WITH CABBAGE

- 5 Lbs of fresh cod fillets
- 1 1/2 Cans of fish sauce
- 1 Small cabbage
- 5 Tbsp butter
- ½ Cup of vegetable stock
- ½ Cup of white wine
- 1 Tsp of ground cumin
- 1 Tomato, cut into wedges
- 8 Slices of bacon
- 1 Bunch of fresh chives

1—Cut the fillets into 6 pieces and season with salt and pepper. Heat the fish sauce in a saucepan, add the fish and let it establish for about 8 minutes over low heat.

2—Arrange the cabbage and cut it firm. Heat the butter in a saucepan and sauté the cabbage for 5 minutes. Then add the vegetable broth and wine and let it establish for about 15 minutes. Seasoning with salt, pepper and cumin.

3—Add the tomatoes to the cabbage. Fry the bacon in a skillet until crisp. Arrange cabbage on plates and finish with codfish fillets. Put a slice of bacon and onion on each plate and place a slice on top of fish.

# COD "A GOMES DE SA" WITH EGGS

- 1 Lbs of Yukon potatoes, peeled and cut into cubes
- 1 Lbs of cod fish, minced
- 2 Medium onions,
- 1 Garlic clove, minced
- 2 Large eggs
- 2 Laurel leafs
- ¼ Cup of Kalamata olives
- Salt and pepper to taste

1—Fill a large pot with cold water, salt, potatoes, eggs cover and let it cook in a medium-low heat for about 20 minutes. Remove from heat and set aside. Crack and peel eggs, separating the yolks from the whites.

2—Fill a medium pot with cold water. Put cod inside the pot, cover and let it cook in a low heat for about 5 to 7 minutes. Remove from heat and set aside.

3—Heat the oil in a skillet over medium low heat, until it shimmers. Add onion, garlic, laurel leafs, salt and pepper. Stir frequently, until browns.

4—In a small bowl mash the yolks with a tablespoon of warm water, until creamy. Cut egg whites into small pieces.

5—Return potatoes to the large pot; add minced cod, onion, creamy egg yolks and egg whites. Mix all together and sprinkle fresh parsley, olives and serve warm.

# Cod "a Bras" with Fries

- 1 Lbs of Yukon potatoes, peeled and cut into small cubes
- 1 Lbs of cod fish, minced
- 1 Large onion, diced
- 1 Garlic clove, minced
- 2 Large eggs
- 1/3 Cup of olive oil
- Kalamata olives
- Fresh parsley
- Salt and pepper to taste

1—Fill a medium pot with cold water. Put cod inside the pot, cover and let it cook in a low heat for about 5 to 7 minutes. Remove from heat and set aside.

2—Meanwhile, heat oil in a large frying pan over medium heat until it shimmers. Peel and cut potatoes into small cubes and fry them for about 3 minutes or until they turn golden brown. Remove from heat and put them aside in a plate with paper towels to absorb extra oil.

3—Heat 2 tablespoons of oil in a large pan over medium low heat, until it shimmers. Add onion, garlic, salt and pepper. Stir frequently, until browns.

4—In a medium bowl beat eggs and add to the onions and garlic. Mixing until they turn into a scramble.

5—In a small bowl mince cod with your fingers. Return potatoes to the large pot; add minced cod, onion, and scramble eggs. Mix all together and sprinkle some olives, fresh parsley and serve warm.

# MEAT AND POULTRY

*Portuguese Beans "Feijoada"*
*My Mom's Roast Chicken*
*Rabbit with Potatoes*
*Pork tenderloin in a Port-fig Sauce*
*Steak with Poached Egg*
*Lamb in a Tawny Port Sauce*
*Veal Scallops in a Lemon Sauce*
*Pork Steaks with Onions*

# Portuguese Beans "Feijoada"

- 2 Lbs dried black beans, picked over and rinsed
- 2 Tbsp of olive oil
- 1 (1-pound) Boneless pork loin, cut into 2-inch slices
- 1 Lbs Beef stew, cut into 2-inch pieces
- 1 Lbs Short ribs cut into 2-inch pieces
- 1 Lbs Carne Seca (Latin cured beef)*
- 1 Lbs linguica or chicken sausage, cut into 2-inch pieces
- 1 Lbs of bacon slab, cut into 4 pieces
- 3 Pork chops (1/2-inch-thick)
- 2 Medium onions, finely chopped (about 3 1/2 cups)
- 4 Garlic cloves, finely chopped
- 3 Tbsp of salt
- 1 Tbsp of freshly ground black pepper
- 2 1/2 Cups of chicken stock

*Carne Seca (Latin cured beef) is available at Latin supermarkets. It can be substituted with Corned beef.

1—In large bowl, combine beans and enough cold water to cover by 2 inches. Let soak in refrigerator overnight. Drain and set aside.

2—In large heavy pot over moderately high heat, heat oil until hot but not smoking. Working in batches, brown pork loin, stew beef, beef short ribs, carne Seca, sausage, bacon, and pork chops, turning occasionally, about 8 minutes per batch. Transfer browned meat to cutting board.

3—Lower heat to moderately low, add onions and garlic to fat in pot, and sauté until onions are soft and translucent, about 8-10 minutes. Add beans, meat, salt, pepper, and chicken broth. Raise heat to high, bring to boil, then lower heat and simmer, covered, until meat is falling off bones, 2 1/2 to 3 hours.

4—Arrange beans in center of large serving platter and surround it with meats. Serve warm with plain rice.

# My Mom's Roast Chicken

- 1 4Lbs chicken
- 6 Tbsp of red pepper paste
- 3 Garlic cloves, minced
- 2 Tbsp of fresh parsley
- 2 to 3 Lbs of Yukon gold potatoes, cut into cubes
- 3 Tbsp of olive oil
- Salt and pepper to taste

1—Heat the oven to 425 degrees. Remove excess fat from the chicken, pat dry and carefully wiggle your fingers under the skin to release from the meat. In a bowl mix 4 tbsp of red pepper paste, garlic, fresh parsley and olive oil. Using your fingers smear the mixture under the skin of the chicken, as well as outside. Salt and pepper to taste.

2—Peel and cut the potatoes and mix them with the rest of the red pepper paste and olive oil. Put chicken in an oiled pan and scatter potatoes around the chicken. Chicken should be breast side up.

3—Roast chicken for about 30 minutes, using tongs, turn the chicken breast down and mix potatoes, so they don't get stuck to the pan. Lower the temperature to 375 degrees and let it cook for another 1 hour—1 ½ hour, turning the bird and mixing potatoes every 20 minutes or so.

4—Remove chicken from the oven and let it rest for about 10 minutes. Grandma Ana cut the chicken into pieces with her own hands. You can cut it, with the kitchen scissors or a knife.

5—Place chicken on a platter, along with the potatoes and serve warm.

# Rabbit with Potatoes

- 2 Lbs Fresh Rabbit, frozen works the same
- 1 Lbs of Yukon golden potatoes, peeled, cut in half's
- ½ Cup of vegetable broth
- 1 Large onion, diced
- 2 Garlic clovers, minced
- 1 Tbsp of fresh rosemary
- 4 Tbsp of olive oil
- 2 Laurel leafs
- Salt and pepper to taste

1—Fill a large pot with cold water, salt, potatoes, cover and let it cook in a medium-low heat for about 20 minutes. Cut Rabbit into pieces (like a chicken).

2—Heat the oil in a skillet over medium low heat, until it shimmers. Add rabbit, onion, garlic, laurel leafs, rosemary, salt and pepper. Stir frequently, until browns. Add vegetable broth, cover and let it simmer for about 25 minutes.

3—Remove rabbit and potatoes from heat, put them in serving plates, and set aside to cool off. Serve rabbit on top of the potatoes with some fresh rosemary. You can serve this dish very hot or just warm.

# Pork tenderloin in a Port-fig Sauce

- 2 to 3 Lbs of pork tenderloins, fat removed
- 3 Tbsp of olive oil
- 10 Dry Figs cut in half's
- ½ Cup of vegetable broth
- 2 Garlic cloves, minced
- 1 Tbsp of brown sugar
- 1 Tsp of fresh ginger, minced
- 1 Cup of ruby port
- 3 Tbsp of fresh cilantro and parsley, chopped
- Salt and pepper to taste

1—Turn on the oven to 450 degrees. Dump the figs in a small saucepan, add the port, vegetable broth, ginger and brown sugar, and bring it to a boil. Reduce the heat, cover, and let it simmer for about 20 minutes. Turn off the heat and let steep for 10 minutes.

2—Seasoned the pork tenderloins with olive oil, salt, pepper and garlic and transfer to a baking sheet. Roast the pork tenderloins until meat thermometer registers 150 degrees, 20 minutes. Transfer tenderloins into a cutting board, cover with aluminum foil, and let it rest for a few minutes.

3—Put the port-fig sauce and stir to pick up the browned bits stuck to the baking sheet, cook to melt the flavors, for 5 minutes. If the sauce its to thin, let it simmer for 3 more minutes. For an elegant serving of the sauce, straining it through a sieve.

4—Cut the pork tenderloins on a diagonal into 1/3-inch slices. Serve the slices warm, drizzle with port-fig sauce, and sprinkle with fresh parsley and cilantro.

# STEAK WITH POACHED EGG

- "A cavalo—on horseback"
- 2 4oz Sirloin steaks
- 3 Garlic cloves, minced
- 3 Tbsp of olive
- 2 Tbsp of butter
- 2 Chicken eggs
- Fresh parsley, chopped
- Salt and pepper to taste

1—Remove steaks from the refrigerator; let them rest at room temperature for 20 minutes. Rub the steaks with butter, salt, pepper and garlic, cover with paper towel, and let them rest for 15 minutes.

2—Heat 2 tablespoons of olive oil, in a large skillet over medium heat until hot. Sear the steaks, working one at the time if necessary, adjusting the heat to avoid burning them, for about 5 minutes per side for medium rare.

3—Heat 1 tablespoon of olive oil, in a medium non-stick skillet over low heat, until hot. Crack in the eggs, season with salt and pepper, fry them sunny side up, 2 minutes.

4—Put the steaks in diner plates, and crown each with a sunny side up egg. Sprinkle meat and eggs with fresh parsley. Serve with French fries.

# Lamb in a Tawny Port Sauce

- 2 ½ Lbs of well-trimmed racks of lamb (each with 8 bones)
- 4 Tbsp of olive oil
- 1/3 cup of red wine
- 1 Garlic clove, minced
- 1 Tbsp of fresh rosemary, minced
- Salt and pepper to taste

**Sauce:**
2 Cups halved seedless red grapes
2 Cups of Tawny Port
1 Cup of low-salt chicken broth
2 Tsp of chopped fresh rosemary
For the sauce

1—Boil all ingredients in large saucepan until reduced to 2 1/3 cups, about 20 minutes. Cool. Puree in blender. Can be made 5 days ahead. Cover and refrigerate, until needed.

**For the Lamb:**
1—Pre-heat the oven at 275 degrees. Remove fat from lamb, and rub with salt, pepper and garlic. Put lamb in a dish, add red wine, and let it sit for 40 minutes.
2—Heat a non-stick skillet with olive oil, until it shimmers. Place lamb in the skillet, until brown, 2 minutes per side. Remove from heat and place skillet in the oven and let it cook for 7 minutes, for medium-rare, 10 minutes for well done.

3—Transfer lamb to platter; let rest 10 minutes. Cut lamb between bones into chops. Set two on each plate. Drizzle sauce, fresh rosemary over the lamb. Serve with roasted potatoes.

# Veal Scallops in a Lemon Sauce

- 8 Veal scallops
- 1 Cup of flour
- 3 Eggs
- 1 Tbsp of milk
- 2/3 Cup of breadcrumbs
- 6 Tbsp of oil
- 8 Anchovy fillets
- 16 Capers
- 1 organically grown lemon
- Salt and pepper to taste

1—Flatten the fillet of veal with a meat hammer. Season veal with salt and pepper to taste. Put flour on a plate. In a second bowl mix eggs with milk and a third dish pour the breadcrumbs.

2—Dip the veal scallops first in flour, then eggs and breadcrumbs. Making sure than all the ingredients adhere well to the meat.

3—Heat the oil in a frying pan and fry the scallops, one by one on both sides during 3 minutes. Remove from skillet and drain on absorbent paper.

4—Wash the lemon with hot water and cut into slices. Serve the scallops garnished with slices of lemon, anchovies and capers. Serve with potato salad.

# Pork Steak with Onions

- 4 Pork steaks
- 3 Onions, cut into rings
- 3 Tbsp of olive oil
- 2 Tbsp of flour
- ½ Cup vegetable broth
- ½ Cup of sherry wine
- 2 Tbsp fresh chives
- Salt and pepper to taste

1—Flatten the steaks with the meat hammer and season with salt and pepper. Peel onions and cut them into rings.

2—Heat the oil in a skillet and auburn both sides of the steaks for about 5 minutes. Put them in an appropriate place to keep warm.

3—Sauté onion rings in olive oil for 3 minutes remaining in the skillet until they are translucent. Sprinkle with flour and pour the vegetable broth and sherry wine.

4—Let the sauce thicken, stirring often. Flavor sauce with chives and serve steaks with onion sauce and mashed potatoes.

# VEGETABLES, EGGS AND OTHERS

*Egg Tortilla with Sausage and French Fries*
*Grandma's Punched Potatoes*
*Broccoli Rabe with Garlic*
*Rice with Cod*
*Ana's Tomato Rice*
*Mashed Potatoes with Almonds*
*Risotto with Pumpkin*
*Portuguese Croquettes*
*Pie with Ham*

# Egg Tortilla with Sausage and French Fries

- 8 Large eggs
- 1 Large Vidalia onion, chopped
- 2 Large Yukon potatoes cut into sticks
- 3 Tbsp of olive oil, or more, if needed
- 3 Small Garlic cloves, minced
- 1 Medium linguica, or dry-cured Spanish chorizo,
- Cut into ¼ inch slices
- ½ Cup of vegetable oil (for fries)
- ¼ Cup of fresh parsley, chopped

**FRENCH FRIES:**

1—Wash and cut the potatoes into sticks. If you don't like the potatoes with skin, peel them and follow the same steps. Drop the potatoes into a bowl with very cold and salty water, for about 5 minutes. Remove potatoes from the water, and pat them dry with paper towels.

2—Heat the vegetable oil in a deep skillet or frying pan, medium-heat until it shimmer. Drop the potatoes into batches. Let them fry for about 6 minutes, until golden.

3—Put each batch of fries in a tray with paper towels, and set aside.

**FOR THE EGGS:**

4—Heat olive oil in a large non-stick skillet, medium-low heat, until it shimmers. Add onions, sausage until light brown. Season with salt and pepper, stirring often, until the onions are translucent, 15 minutes.

5—Beat eggs in a medium bowl until fluffy and season with salt, pepper and 1 tablespoon of fresh parsley.

6—Drop the French fries into the skillet, and pour in the egg mixture on top. Using a rubber spatula, quick stir the eggs and fries. Jiggle the skillet to settle contents. Run the spatula around sides of the skillet to release tortilla, until gold brown, 3 to 4 minutes.

7—Remove skillet from heat. Slide a large plate on top of the skillet and flip over the tortilla into the plate. Return skillet to the heat and slide tortilla back into the skillet, let it cook for 3 or 4 minutes. Make sure eggs are cooked through.

8—Slide the tortilla into a large platter and sprinkle with the remaining fresh parsley. Or serve it right from the pan.

# GRANDMA'S PUNCHED POTATOES

- 2 Lbs of tiny potatoes, like rainbow potatoes,
- (Pricked with a fork, all around)
- 1/ 2 Cup of olive oil
- 4 to 6 Garlic cloves, sliced
- 1 Lbs of rock salt or very coarse salt

1—Rinse the potatoes with cold water, pat them dry and pricked them with a fork. Put 3 tablespoons of the olive oil in a bowl and drop the potatoes, roll them in olive oil.

2—In a deep iron pot or a pan that can handle big amounts of salt. Heat 4 tablespoon of oil, until it shimmers, add garlic, cook until golden. Drop potatoes into the iron pot, and cover potatoes with salt.

3—Cover iron pot, lower heat to medium-low and let then cook for about 45 to 50 minutes.

4—When the potatoes are done, remove them form salt. Before serving the potatoes, press on them with your finger, wrist or mallet to split. Drizzle potatoes with olive oil, fresh garlic and serve hot.

# Broccoli Rabe with Garlic

- 3 Bunch's fresh Broccoli Rabe
- 1 Head of Garlic cloves cut in half's
- 1/3 Cup of olive oil
- 1 Tsp of red pepper flakes
- Salt and pepper to taste

1—Fill a large pot with water and salt. Bring to a boil over high heat. As soon as the water boils, drop the broccoli Rabe, cover, and cook for about 4 minutes. Using a fork or tongs, transfer broccoli to a bowl with paper towels to absorb the excess water.

2—Heat the oil in a large skillet, over medium heat, until it shimmers. Add garlic and let it sizzle, stirring frequently, until golden brown.

3—Add broccoli to the skillet and cook, turning frequently with a fork or tongs. Let them cook for about 5 to 6 minutes, until tender.

Serve warm, and season with salt, pepper and pepper flakes.

# RICE WITH COD

- 750g Shredded cod
- 100g Rice
- 2 Ripe tomatoes, peeled
- 1 Small onion, chopped
- 1 Green pepper, cut into strips
- 1 Small garlic head
- 1 Laurel leaf
- 1 Bunch of fresh cilantro
- 1.5 dl of olive oil
- 2 Cups of water
- Salt and pepper to taste

1—Make a stew with olive oil, onion and garlic until it begins to blond. Add the tomatoes, bay leaves, peppers cut into strips, and soaked cod, smashed, peeled and without bones. Let cook well.

2—Add rice, salt and water to the stew, mix well and simmer for 5 minutes. Keep the pan closed for five more minutes and place fresh and chopped cilantro. Serve piping hot.

# ANA'S TOMATO RICE

- 2 Cups of white rice
- 3 Tbsp of olive oil
- 1 Onion, chopped
- 2 Bay leafs
- 2 Garlic cloves, chopped
- 4 Large Plum tomatoes, seeded and diced
- 4 Cups of chicken or vegetable stock (water works, too)
- Salt and pepper to taste

1—Heat the oil in a medium saucepan, at medium-low heat until it shimmers. Add onions, garlic and bay leaf, until the onions get golden color.

2—Add the tomatoes and cook for about 4 minutes, mixing often. Pour in the stock and bring it to a boil.

3—Add rice, reduce heat to low and cook, covered, until the rice is tender, and all the liquid evaporated, 10 to 15 minutes. Tomato rice needs a bit more time to cook than regular rice.

4—Toss out the bay leaves and serve rice hot.

# MASHED POTATOES WITH ALMONDS

- 1-½ Lbs of Yukon potatoes cut in half
- 1/4 Cup chopped almonds
- 3 Tbsp butter, room temperature
- 1 Bunch of fresh dill
- 1/2 Cucumber
- Fresh Nutmeg, grated
- Salt and pepper to taste

1—Wash the potatoes and bake with skin in the oven at 200 degrees for 40 minutes. Toast 1 tablespoon of almonds in butter until golden. Remove them immediately from the pan and let them cool. Reduce almonds to half and mashed into pure. The remaining chops coarsely.

2—Chop the dill coarsely. Peel the cucumber, cut it lengthwise and scrape the seeds with a teaspoon and cut it into very tiny cubes.

3—Let the potatoes cool slightly, cut them in half and with a small spoon, scrape the inside. Mash with a fork, the potato pulp with the remaining butter. Mix with the chopped almonds and the almonds reduced to pure and carefully incorporate the diced cucumber and dill. Season mashed potatoes with salt, pepper and fresh nutmeg.

# Risotto with Pumpkin

- 3 Cups of vegetable stock
- 1 Small onion, finely chopped
- ½ Lbs of pumpkin flesh, grated
- 1 Tbsp olive oil
- 1 Tbsp of sage, chopped at the time
- 1 1/3 Cup of Arborio rice
- 2/3 Cup of Parmesan cheese, grated
- Salt and pepper to taste

1—Heat the broth in a saucepan and simmer for a while. Grate the flesh of the pumpkin. Heat oil in large saucepan and sauté onion until translucent. Add the pumpkin and let it establish for 5 minutes. Sprinkle with sage and add the rice, stirring constantly. Continue to stir until the rice is well engaged in oil.

2—Pour 2/3 of the broth and stir until rice has absorbed all the liquid. Add more broth and stir until it is absorbed too. Continue to add the remaining liquid until the rice is cooked and released. Finally, enter the cheese and season with salt and pepper. Serve the risotto with grated Parmesan cheese.

# Portuguese Croquettes

- 6 Large Yukon Potatoes
- 1 Large onion, finely chopped
- 2 Apples, finely chopped
- 2 Eggs
- ½ Tsp of sugar
- 1 ¼ Cup of flour, more for work
- 4 Tbsp of olive oil
- Salt and pepper to taste

1—Wash the potatoes and boil them in water seasoned with salt for about 25 minutes. Drain and let cool slightly. Then remove skin from the potatoes and pass them in a blender or crush them.

2—Peel the onion and apples. Chop the onion finely, remove the center of apples and chop them finely. Mix the apples, potatoes, flour, salt, eggs, sugar and knead very well.

3—Keep adding flour to hands and working surface, this way the mixture will not stick. Form the dough into rolls the length of a finger and rinse them in a little flour, before cooking. Meanwhile, preheat the oven to 160 degrees.

4—Heat 2 Tbsp oil in a medium saucepan, at a medium-low heat until it shimmers. Quickly drop croquettes until blondish. Then brush with remaining oil and bake for about 30 minutes.

# PIE WITH HAM

- 1 Bag of Pasta (your choice)
- ½ Lbs of Ham
- 4 Oz of Gouda cheese
- 4 Oz of béchamel sauce
- ½ Cup of milk
- 4 Oz of cheese to melt
- 3 Tbsp of fresh chives
- Salt and pepper to taste

1—Cook pasta in hot water for about 10 to 12 minutes, until al dente. Then, drain it well. Preheat oven to 225 degrees. Cut the ham and grate. Cut cheese and Gouda into cubes. Take the béchamel sauce with milk to a boil, add the cheese to melt and mix. If necessary, add salt and pepper.

2—Make alternate layers of pasta and ham in a previously greased pan. Cover the layers with the sauce. To finish, cover the pie with the sauce left over, sprinkle with cheese, bake in the second position from the bottom and bake for 20 minutes. Serve the pie warm and sprinkled with fresh chives.

# DESSERTS

*Pasteis de Chaves (Keys Pastry)*
*Cinnamon and Sugar Fritters*
*Snowballs*
*Creamy Eggs with Sherry*
*Snow of Milk with Sour Cherries*
*Pears in Port Wine*
*Portuguese Cream Tarts*
*White Chocolate Mousse*
*Rice Pudding*

# PASTEIS DE CHAVES
# (KEYS PASTRY)

**PASTRY:**
- 8 Cups of all-purpose flour
- 2 Tsp of white vinegar
- 2 Tsp of extra virgin olive oil
- Juice of 1 lemon
- 1 1/4—1 1/3 cups of hot water
- Flour for work surface and hands

**FILLING:**
- 3 Tbsp of olive oil
- ½ Lbs of beef, ground
- 1 Medium onion, minced
- 2 Garlic cloves, minced
- ¼ Cup of dry white wine
- ¼ Cup of chicken broth
- ½ Tbsp of fresh parsley, minced

1—Add 6 cups of flour to a large bowl (the remaining 2 cups will be used when rolling out the dough). Make a well in the center and add water (start with 1 cup) and vinegar. Combine with a fork. Add the olive oil and continue mixing, adding more water if needed to make soft dough.

2—Turn the dough out onto a floured surface and knead by hand, oiling hands if needed, until the dough is soft, malleable, and smooth, about 10 minutes.

3—Divide the dough into 18-20 equal pieces and roll (rolling pin or pasta machine) each piece out to a rough oval shape, about 18-19 inches across, sprinkling the work surface and phyllo with flour to keep from sticking. Wrap in plastic wrap and refrigerate overnight before using.

4—Heat the olive oil in a large skillet or wok over medium heat until hot. Lower the heat to medium-low and add onion, garlic, beef and cook, breaking up the meat with a wooden spoon, stirring frequently. Add wine, broth and let it simmer, until wine and broth evaporates almost completely.

5—Remove saucepan form the heat and season beef with salt, pepper and fresh parsley and set aside and let it cool completely. Remove phyllo dough from refrigerator 10 to 15 minutes before using it. Pre-heat the oven at 400 degrees.

6—Roll out 1 pastry sheet on lightly floured surface to 12-inch square. Place 1/8 of beef mixture on bottom half of 1 square. Brush pastry edges with water. Fold unfilled half of pastry over filling, forming half moons. Press edges of pastry closed with tines of fork or your fingers.

7—Place pastry on large baking sheet. Repeat with remaining pastry and beef mixture. Bake pastries 5 minutes. Reduce heat to 375 degrees. Bake pastries until puffed and golden brown, about 15 minutes longer. Serve warm with an espresso or latte.

# Cinnamon and Sugar Fritters

**Sugar with cinnamon:**
- 1 Cup of organic sugar
- 1 Tbsp of cinnamon
- ½ Tsp of ginger, powder

**Fritters:**
- 2 Cups of white flour
- 2 Large eggs
- ½ Cup of pumpkin, cooked, mashed
- ½ Cup of milk
- ½ Cup of vegetable oil
- Salt to taste

1—In a small bowl or deep soup plate, mix sugar, cinnamon and ginger. Set aside until fritters are done.

2—In a deep bowl, beat the eggs and sugar, with a stand mixer or by hand, until gets creamy and fluffy. Add pumpkin, milk and flour ½ cup at the time. Mix well and let it rest for 5 minutes.

3—Heat the vegetable oil in a large skillet or wok over medium-low heat until hot. Working in batches, drop the batter by tablespoons in the hot skillet Fry until golden brown and cooked through, to 2 minutes per side.

4—Transfer fritters to paper towels to drain. Add more vegetable oil to the skillet, as needed.

5—Coat a large serving dish with the cinnamon mixture. Transfer the fritters to the serving dish, and drizzle with cinnamon mixture. Repeat until you finish fritters. Serve warm or room temperature.

# Snowballs

- 2/3 Cups of water
- 4 Tbsp of butter
- A pinch of salt
- 11/2 Cup of flour
- 3 Eggs

## For the filling and dusting:
- 2 Cups of whipped sweet cream
- Powdered sugar

1—Boil the water with butter and salt. Remove from heat and pour all the flour at once, smashing everything in electric or hand mixer. Bring the pot back to heat and work the dough until it comes off the walls of the pan.
2—Place the ball of dough in a bowl of high walls and mix eggs immediately beating with electric or hand mixer. Let the dough cool.
3—For a softer dough add the remaining eggs one by one continuing until the dough has a glossy surface.
4—With a tablespoon place mass clump 12-15 regular sizes in a floured tray. Take the preheated oven for 30 to 40 minutes. After cooking, cut the cake with a knife and let cool.
5—Fill with whips cream and sprinkle with powdered sugar and serve then right away.

# CREAMY EGGS WITH SHERRY

- 2 Whole eggs
- 4 Egg yolks
- 2 Tbsp of vanilla sugar
- 2 Tbsp of sugar
- 2 Tbsp of sherry

1—Beat the whole eggs with egg yolks, sugar and vanilla sugar. Cook eggs and sugar in a water-bath, stirring constantly. Pour the sherry little by little until you have formed a thick cream.

2—Serve immediately in tall glasses or desert cups. Serve with almond cookies.

# Snow of Milk with Sour Cherries

- 2 Cups of whole milk
- ¼ Cup of starch
- 1/3 Cup of sugar
- 2 Whole eggs
- 1 Small jar of sour Cherry preserves
- Lemon zest
- Juice of 1 Small Lemon
- 1 Tsp of Aguardente (brandy)

1—Add all ingredients in a saucepan bring them to the water bath and beat vigorously until a thick cream form.

2—Allow cooling, stirring constantly. Put the well-drained cherries in bowls or tall glasses and watering them with cream.

# PEARS IN PORT WINE

- 6 Large pears, peeled
- ½ Cup of Port wine
- 1 ½ Cup of brown sugar
- 4 Cinnamon sticks
- 1 Orange
- 1 Tbsp of Lavender honey

1—Put the pears onto a deep pan. Add port wine, cinnamon sticks, sugar, orange juice and peel.

2—Cook a low heat until pears gets soft, 6 to 8 minutes, and with a wine/ orange color. When cooked, remove pears from the pan, putt them in a serving dish, and set aside.

3—Leave the pan with the liquid in the low heat. Add honey, mixing constantly, until it turns into syrup. Remove syrup from heat.

4—Drizzle pears with the port wine syrup and serve warm. Alone or with ice cream.

# Portuguese Cream Tarts

**For pastry:**
- 1 Package frozen puff pastry (2 sheets)
- 1 Tbsp of butter, melted
- For custard filling:
- 1 Cup granulated sugar
- 2 Tbsp of all-purpose flour
- 2 1/2 cups Heavy cream
- Finely grated zest of 1 small lemon (about 1 tsp)
- 8 Large egg yolks
- 1/4 Tsp salt
- 1 Tsp vanilla

**For topping:**
1 Tsp confectioner's sugar
1/2 Tsp cinnamon

1—Partially thaw pastry just until sheets can be unfolded but dough is still quite stiff. Gently unfold 1 sheet and cut along folds, forming 3 equal strips. Repeat with remaining pastry sheet.

2—Turn each strip on its side (cut side up) and coil tightly to form a flat 2 inch-wide spiral. On a lightly floured surface, press spiral with heel of your hand to flatten into a 3-inch round.

3—Lightly grease muffin cups with melted butter. Place each round in a muffin cup and press into bottom and side, lining cup to within 1/8 inch of top.

4—Preheat oven to 450°F. Whisk together sugar and flour in a 3-quart heavy saucepan, then whisk in remaining filling ingredients and cook over moderate heat, stirring constantly, until first bubble appears on surface, about 10 minutes (custard will get thick).

5—Transfer custard to a bowl and cool, whisking occasionally, until just warm, about 15 minutes, then fill pastry cups with custard, about 2 tablespoons each.

6—Bake tarts in upper third of oven until pastry is deep golden, 10 to 12 minutes.

7—Cool tarts slightly in pans on a rack, about 10 minutes, then lift from pans using a small offset spatula or dull knife. Sift confectioner's sugar, then cinnamon, over tarts and serve warm or at room temperature.

# WHITE CHOCOLATE MOUSSE

- 3 Large eggs
- 1 Cup of cream, plus 2 Tbsp
- 6 Oz of white chocolate
- ¼ Cup of sugar
- Chocolate sauce

1—Separate the egg whites and egg yolks. Beat the egg whites and cream until stiff. Melt chocolate in double boiler, stirring constantly.

2—Beat the egg yolks until foamy consistency. Mix the sugar with the melted chocolate before it withdrew from the bath. Then, start by carefully engaging the cream, then the egg whites with the chocolate mixture.

3—Pour the mousse in a glass bowl and chill the refrigerator overnight. To serve, spoon to make balls of ice cream. Distribute them with chocolate sauce.

# Rice Pudding

- 1 2/3 Cup of long grain rice
- 1½ Cups of milk
- 1½ Tbsp of butter
- 4 Large eggs
- 1/3 Cup of sugar
- 2 Tbsp of vanilla sugar
- 1 Tsp of lemon zest
- 1/2 Tsp of nutmeg
- 1/2 Tsp of ground cinnamon
- 2½ Oz of raisins
- Butter for greasing

1—Cook the rice in salted water by following the instructions on the package and let cool. Best to cook the rice the day before.

2—Preheat the oven to 160 degrees. Mix the milk with the remaining ingredients (except rice) in a bowl. Finally, integrate the rice to the mixture.

3—Grease a pie dish and pour the rice mixture into it. Return to oven to bake for about 60 minutes, or until the dough is firm. Remove pie from oven and let cool for 20 minutes. Serve while hot. If you like, serve with stewed fruit.

# INDEX

## A

## B

## C

## E

## F

# Would you like to see your manuscript become a book?

**If you are interested in becoming a PublishAmerica author, please submit your manuscript for possible publication to us at:**

**acquisitions@publishamerica.com**

**You may also mail in your manuscript to:**

**PublishAmerica
PO Box 151
Frederick, MD 21705**

---

## We also offer free graphics for Children's Picture Books!

---

# www.publishamerica.com

CPSIA information can be obtained at www.ICGtesting.com
Printed in the USA
BVOW070658081212

307646BV00002B/16/P